Phases of the Moon

Also by Lynn Kozma

Catching the Light
Great South Bay

Phases of the Moon

Lynn Kozma

Papier-Mache Press
Watsonville CA

ISBN: 0-918949-47-5 Softcover

ISBN: 0-918949-48-3 Hardcover

Cover art by Lynn Zachreson
Cover design by Cynthia Heier
Photograph by Pat Magee
Typography by Prism Photographics

Grateful acknowledgment is made to the following publications which first published some of the material in this book:

Albatross, 1990 for "By the Pond's Edge"; *Midwest Poetry Review,* January 1990 for "My Father"; *Long Island Quarterly*, Spring 1991 for "Great Blue Heron"; *Long Island Quarterly*, Summer 1991 for "Return to Cutchogue"; *Live Poets,* Spring 1992 for "A Week in the Woods"; *Long Island Quarterly*, Fall 1992 for "Fatal Attraction"; *Color Wheel,* Spring 1993 for "At the Dock" and "Sanctuary"; *The Small Pond,* Spring 1993 for "Great South Bay"; *Midwest Poetry Review,* April 1993 for "Living with Ghosts"; and *Great South Bay* (Birnham Wood Graphics, 1993) for "High Tide," "Cardinal," "Carp," "Saw Whet Owl," "Space," "Salvation," "Praying Mantis," "Shadow Lines," "Sound Effects," "Indian Pipes," "In the Fall," "Crickets," "At First Light," "Soundings," "Traveler," "Promises," "Questions," and "Sentience."

Library of Congress Cataloging-in-Publication Data

Kozma, Lynn, 1919-
    Phases of the moon / Lynn Kozma.
       p.   cm.
    ISBN 0-918949-48-3 (acid-free) : $12.00 — ISBN 0-918949-47-5 (pbk. : acid-free) : $8.00
    I. Title.
    PS3561.093P48   1993
    811'.54—dc20   94-2577
                                                CIP

For Pat
who loved poetry

Thanks to:
The editors at Papier-Mache Press—Sandra Martz and Shirley Coe—for their direction, expertise, and interest in this collection.

Elaine Preston, Nancy Hall, Richard Gambrell, Ellen Pickus, and Mindy Kronenberg for their time and effort in reviewing this book.

George Wallace, of Birnham Wood Graphics, for publishing *Great South Bay*, a mini-chapbook, in which several poems in Part One of this book appeared.

My faithful poetry group, which is an active outgrowth of a workshop at Hofstra University in 1988—Therese McPhilliamy, Ellen Pickus, Frank Van Zant, and more recently Elaine Preston—for their invaluable critiques and support.

My husband, Bill, for his patience.

The muse, for staying with me.

Contents

Phases of the Moon

At the Dock

At the Dock

All I need to do
is be still, and the answer
will come. Weightless, I listen
for some profound reply
to a question that cannot be named.
In the hush of changing light
rafts of eelgrass drift by
on incoming tide. A tern drops
like a stone into flashing water,
emerges with its silver prize.
Mallards float soundlessly
toward the bay.

Lying flat on old weathered boards
I stare at flying clouds until
it seems the dock and I are moving.
I hold onto the piling, afraid of
falling off the earth's edge.

Cicadas have ended their chorus
for the day. Fireflies blossom into
sparks. An occasional plane drones
overhead, so high it might be a visitor
from another planet. A setting sun
drains the last light away, and the dark
bowl of sky is pricked by early stars.

Still I lie there in some deep
state of peace, treasuring each moment
as though it will never come again.
And it never will. And that is the answer
I have waited for, given silently,
flowing inward like the tide.

High Tide

I watch
   the blue crab
      on the piling
beneath the gauzy
   waterline
     selecting barnacles
prying them apart
   delving inside
     with his pincers
the victim extending
   soft orange arms
     in futile defense.
The end comes quickly
   empty shells gape open
     the predator moves on.

I want that crab to know
   that agony transfers itself
     to other living things
so I kick the dock's post
   watch him scurry deeper
     out of sight.

Death is like this—pinching
   eating its victims whole.
     It happens every day.
But for a moment I feel omnipotent
   stamping my foot
     making Death disappear.

Phases of the Moon

Bright moon stares
from the great bowl of sky
sailing weightless
glowing with cold fire
impersonal as a stranger.
We say it shows the face
of a man, is made of green
cheese, sheds its skin,
or covetous, steals
the sun's fire. One day
we calculate its distance
from earth, arrive on its
rocky, cratered plains,
at once dispel the mystery.

I prefer the inaccessible moon,
the maddening phantom moon,
the cabalistic, lopsided slipstream
Queen of Night, disappearing,
born again whole and new,
silvering my skin, turning
my heart back fifty years
to a dance in the woods
under its spell, aflame with
my first mad
                fall
                        into love.

Heat Wave

Sizzling, steaming,
the burnt-out sun
slides from a blistered sky
toward certain death
in the boiling sea.

Sparrows, too stressed to sing,
huddle in dark spaces.
Carp rise in slow motion
to snatch a lazy dragonfly.

Cicadas, emerging from a former
life, hang their old bodies
on drooping trees, at once
begin a strident complaint.
A few weary fireflies signal
another breathless night.

We fill the birdbath
for the third time since dawn,
draw drapes against evening heat.
Listless and dull, we try
to imagine glaciers, a white
winter day, the sky a thunderous
shade of grey.

Late Summer, Late Afternoon

I walk through fields
of feather grass bleached
white by lowering sun.
Butterfly weed explodes
in a silent barrage
of silken parachutes filled
with incredible light.
Gold defines every twig
on the bayberry, which
lives forever in nothing
but sand.

The last zinnia holds
a chilled bumblebee.
Receding tide, hurrying
toward sunset, lips
bulkheads, and in a watery
voice promises to return
tomorrow. Two mallards
star the inlet. I feel
wealthy before this harvest
of light, touch each leaf
in passing, the power
of Midas in my hands.

The Dream Time

Evening is slowly invented
by a mockingbird's litany,
the last stanza of a robin's poem.

Gulls slide silently toward
a drowning sun. The bee seeks
a flower's heart. Marigolds fade

in the anonymous absence of light.
The sleeping dog runs in her dreams.
Lying awake, I float in crosscurrents

of time, review my former lives,
discover who I have become,
fall in love with night.

The Swan

There should be a flourish
of trumpets, waving banners, a symphony
to announce his arrival on the shining
water. Scattering Canadas, he settles
regally, folded wings held high.
Eyes glittering, he hisses
at my approach—warily accepts
my offering of bread.

I yearn to become small enough
to lie between those white wings.
Holding on to his graceful neck
I would glide with him in silent majesty,
bound with the melody of trust.
Then, with a sudden surge of power
we would rise through blue air
into the crystal morning, and our
flight would last
forever.

Cyprinus Carpio

What do they do all winter
    beneath the flat grey ice
        submerged in great darkness?

Do they sink into profound sleep
    dreaming mayflies, moving water?
        At what unnamed moment will they

surface through murky water
    stretch their long silky bodies
        taste the air with pouting mouths?

April again, and I was there
    watched their first tentative rising.
        Seeing me they dove quickly

remembering last summer's lures,
    hooks, shadows, chance
        of fatal carelessness.

Am I imbuing them
    with some instructed light
        they cannot feel?

I want to believe
    in the nexus between us,
        the moment

of pure sight when we read
    each other's mind—
        and I do.

Osprey

Requiring heights for safety and command
he arrives through blue air silently
to clutch the jagged edge of a storm-killed
tree with his fish-trap claws. The wind's
fingers ruffle his snowy breast.

Imperious, ruby eyed, elegant,
the dark and light of him proclaims
pure majesty, dominion over inlet,
river, every small fish in the sea.

We rush for the camera, praying
he will stay—crawl to the opened door
to focus, fix the lens, freeze him
forever. He preens and poses.

Now, he lives within a frame, catches
the light from searching sun, flickering hearth.
I fill my eyes with his happiness.

Priorities

Birds fill me with wonder.
Snakes, however, slithering
unexpectedly over my shoes,
obsidian eyes alight with menace,
tongues flicking fire, are not
creatures I would miss.

But yesterday, in soft spring,
a young one, bold enough to cross
the naked road, became a victim
of bolder birds harassing him
with stiletto bills until he
coiled and recoiled to escape.

I quickly intervened on behalf
of that least-loved life—drove
the greedy cardinals to high branches.
That snake's writhings became my own.
I carried his tan body to deep leaves
while he played dead, which for him
was the safest thing to do.

True, I interfered with Nature.
But who wouldn't want to be saved
having been born, brand new,
into the dazzling world
of summer?

First Snow

I climb a ragged hill,
enter thick woods. Trees
with broken arms lift
their arthritic bones
scratching a grey sky.

The world is silence
marred by the crunch
of my boots, conversation
of spent leaves.

I am Eve in a white Eden,
Artemis with her bow,
a druid worshipping the spirit
within an oak.

Suddenly I feel miscast
on this sacred stage.
My breath disturbs
the pure air.

Voiceless, a splintered finger
points the way back, directing
me across the hill's spine
to the other side
of the world.

Shadow Lines

That timeless moment
when the moonlight moved
changing each angle
of the barn's roof,
holds me suspended
between yesterday
and tomorrow.

The smooth stones of time
slide past without sound,
leave a hollow sense
of loss. I reach for
your hand, listen
to a dog's complaint,
watch swirling fog,
finding in one moment
an excess of light
called *Now,* and *Now,*
and *Now.*

Winter

Birds crowd feeders,
battle each other
for prime positions,
nudge the competition
off and away, chatter
ceaselessly, then rise
like a cloud of confetti
to the harbor of hemlocks,
wondering what became
of the benevolent sun,
warm blue air.

One day, as things change,
I shall learn the pecking
order, fly at lightning
speed, wear iridescent
clothes, sing rhapsodies.

How dull earthlings
will seem to me then,
plodding along, afraid
of the cold, living
in shadows, rooted
like trees.

Symphony

The world is made of ice.
Pines speak
in shattering whispers
to the willows
who toss their long glass hair
in the wind.

Lifeless leaves rustle
their dry grief.
With muted voice
gulls question the wind
wheeling through mist,
shadow against shadow.

The world is still,
holding its hoary breath.
Music sweeps the treetops
in a symphony of winter,
flinging crystal notes
against a milk-glass sky.

I dream of summer,
and one firefly.

Promises

All winter I check the garden
    staring at the site
    where jack-in-the-pulpit
emerges each spring.

Through March and April
    there is no sign, and I think
    he will not come again,
remembering fall floods, glaze

of ice, squirrels' frantic digging
    for sustenance. Then, like a shout,
    one May morning he is there,
standing triumphant.

The papery bloom lasts only a week,
    abiding by the rules.
    All that effort
for one flickering taste of light!

And I think of the driving force
    behind the hard smack of salmon
    flinging themselves upstream
over and over. And all of us

fighting to stay alive
    holding on
    through patchwork winters
uncountable dawns,

believing in the power
    behind the raging sea,
    behind the surge
of each perennial bloom.

Traveler

The butterfly emerges
  like a bit of blown taffeta,
    clings to her chrysalis

sways in warm sun,
  amazed at form and color,
    spreads her pleated wings.

At once her life depends
  on the beckoning face of flowers,
    a carrying breeze in autumn.

This miracle occurs outside
  our usual vision—a tantalizing
    segment of summer.

In my life's bondage
  I shall never own her grace
    or know her secrets.

Rooted to the ground, I am
  colorless, insecure,
    afraid to try my wings,

while she, complete, incomparable,
  sips nectar, enchants us,
    a drifter on the wind.

Skeletons

I pass those dead limbless trees
each morning, every day, month, year
since that rapist storm disrobed them,
tossed their clothes like old rags
over the swirl of a rising tide,
salting fragile roots, splitting
their creaking hearts like ax
on firewood.

Five years ago—and still they stand
unbending, grey spires carved
against the blue—lonely sentinels
staring with blind eyes
for sails on the bay.

I am impatient with their patience
to persevere—their silent strength.
Are they reminders of how we must
endure? Does the summer contrast,
grey on green, teach us how to see?

Cardinal

Some trick of vision,
refraction of light, familiar
branches etched against blue sky
prompted his choice
of the lower path, most direct,
straight into barrier glass.

He dropped like a flaming stone,
lay stunned on a world of leaves,
attempting to regain his breath of life.
The glory of a few bright feathers
waved lazily on the pane.

I carried him, trembling, through
a house he had never entered,
to a leafy shelf outside,
placed branches for his feet,
said a few soft words. His black
eyes glittered into mine.

Never mind all the others, flying,
chattering at feeders. I wanted
that bird to live—the one I had
held like a sacrament in my hand.

Suddenly, alert, he was off
to the nearest tree, leaving behind
a sound like happiness, the fire
of being alive.

Appearing, Disappearing

After heavy rain
    the bountiful endless
        vengeful kind

weird forms emerge
    overnight from the sand:
        five-pointed black

stars with grey centers
    clutching cold pebbles
        with charred fingers

blossoming like fragments
    of some galactic
        long-lost world.

Are they alien visitors
    telling silent secrets
        we cannot comprehend

or a wild scattered happiness
    born of water
        flaming in the dark?

September

Every few hours
I view the dusty miller
to see if the praying mantis
has moved. The lacy silver
leaves have sheltered her
for half the summer.

Sometimes, the mantis's fragile
arms are folded tight, like an old
woman renouncing life, or
extended rigidly, ready to strike
a fearless fly or fat cricket
venturing over the brown shoulders
of soil and wood chips.

She has taught me this:
how she swivels that Martian head;
that her bulging green eyes
see everything; that after mating,
in some quixotic ecstasy,
she bites off her lover's head.
Later, she lays a froth of eggs,
an impervious commitment
to continuity.

After days of mutual surveillance
what does she know about me?

Any Moment

we thought the house
would burn, windows
shatter from the heat
of a sun hurling fire
across the bay, bathing
all things in a glow
so intense we closed our
eyes against the flames.

Will the waters turn
to vapor, distant stars
grow dim? When night
fades into light
will the scenery
be changed?

Chased by a searing sun
the world, one day
will change, become
a shadow on the moon.
Until then, watch
the orange sea,
the glory fade
too soon.

Great South Bay

Wading waist-high
    in blue-green water
        we learn to clam with our feet.

Moving slowly, casually,
    we begin to discern
        what is hard whole clam,

what is empty shell,
    plunging arms deep,
        finger-scooping the prize.

The clam, I suppose,
    has his own sense of justice,
        different from ours,

which is why he tries
    to escape, clenching his shell,
        burrowing deeper.

But we win, of course,
    judging our needs
        to be greater than his.

Soon we are part
    of the flowing eelgrass,
        the great bowl of sky.

For a short summer hour
    our shadows move on the water,
        dipping and rising like gulls.

Salvation

Describing a perfect circle
over and over, the lone mallard
dips her yellow bill into blue-grey
water, facing the end of the world.

Starving, she edges closer
to the shore. Sun strikes sparks
from metal hanging loosely
out of a tight mouth. Softly,
quietly, I lower a dip net,
raise her, exhausted, from the inlet,
gentle her to the weathered wood.

Her feathers lie still as morning,
onyx eyes imploring, as I snip
the pronged hook in two, restore
her to sweet freedom, then slide
easily into her joy of deliverance.

Does she sometimes think
of my hands, my voice,
that breath-of-life day?

Fatal Attraction

The first chill of autumn
    and dragonflies bloom
        over misty pond.
Filled with sun and vanity
    they hover low to see themselves
        in the flat, dark mirror.
Gauzy winged, prismatic,
    they turn the water
        to a multitude of rainbows.

I watched this extravagant display,
    a final summer ballet,
        knowing how it would end:
The shining carp rose like missiles
    out of the pond's silo,
        unable to resist the lure,
creating a symphony of motion,
        perfected, unrehearsed.

Then it was over, circles
    meeting circles,
        glassy surface still.
Some escape
    to cling trembling
        in the harbor of reeds.

It happens every fall—
    dragonflies charmed by their images—
        narcissus.

Riot

In the lightning-flickered dark
a vandal raids our sleep
with rowdy rumblings
clamoring the air—
strides dark streets
in iron boots, splits
sullen sky to let the deluge
through, tears pale petals
from new blooms, pounding
earth raw—an anarchist.

Powerless before his might
we cringe, cover our ears
at each thunderclap, protect
our eyes against unnatural light.

The wren, caught between
night and day, has greater
faith—holds the candle
of his song before him
like an acolyte.

Storm with No Name

Out of thick night
a pencil line of dawn is quickly erased.
Barometers fall. Trees sway and bend
before rushing wind.

And on the pebbled path
leading toward us in the vulnerable house
a glistening liquid snake of light advances,
seeks swales, nudges stones aside,

arrives quickly drowning everything
in sight, then meets an arm of itself, turning
roads to canals, hissing through submerged ground,
becoming a wide swirling lake.

This flood has a mind
of its own, lord of all, dwarfing our triumphs.
And we know that the flat white impersonal moon
will, in time, pull the water away.

There is nothing we can do.
Nothing we can say.

Crickets

know they are to blame
for singing the world
into winter. Their steady
chorus effectively turns us
away from the sun.
This astounding feat
results in blackened vines,
disappearing bees, bare
trees. Silent with guilt
crickets move slowly
on hardening earth, seek
refuge in bleached grasses,
burrow on weakened legs,
attempt invisibility.

But crickets, in winter
will not leave my thoughts.
Inventing them in corners,
their voices dividing silence
from silence, I know they are
planning the next move.

Hatching unseen without
the power to sing, they change
penurious winter into
extravagant spring.

Sound Effects

Listening, I hear the unexpected:
Ivy hisses, creeping up defenseless trunks.
New grass pipes through warmed soil.
Leaves whisper old secrets. Moss,
springing between red bricks, hums
long-lost tunes. Ceaseless chatter
of dandelions floods blue air.
    Stones chant, hollow as drums.

I am dizzy with voices,
incessant clamor. Bracing myself
against the moving earth
I am powerless to stop
    the surge and swell.

All of this happened
the day you said listen to the ocean roar,
and handed me a glistening, washed clean
    pure white singing shell.

Sentience

I know
    that in Nature
        many things are flawed:

stunted trees
    birds with one leg
        babies born blind.

But I need to believe
    it will all come right
        some sweet night

when the owl snaps open
    her wings, flies with faith
        toward a rising moon.

Which means we may not
    always understand
        the Grand Design.

We can only try
    not to be afraid
        to spread our imperfect wings

and fly with the owl
    toward a new mysterious
        circle of light.

Indian Pipes

Sinuous, translucent,
something dreamed,
this primordial sight
breaks through damp ground
to stand thick fingered,
blushing in sudden light.

Fashioned of lightning
and soft rain, they speak
of sultry nights
when ghosts glide
in moon's cold glare—
smell of decay
and the same quick spark
that started the beat
of man's heart.

I leave the mystery
of their presence
to the trees' shade,
the powdering bark—
expecting, when night
descends, to see
their smoking bowls
glow in the dark.

Great Blue Heron

Carved against a background
of new green he stands motionless,
   neck extended, reading the shallow pond.

With lightning speed his yellow beak
stabs the water, surfaces with a struggling
   black and gold fish.

Immobile again, he waits
until the contest ends, tilts his head,
   swallows, resumes his vigilance.

These things happen. Birds snatch
butterflies in midair; shards of light
   pierce the dark; trees catch the moon.

Between us
one sharp word
   can kill.

By the Pond's Edge

Watch the water
collared with froth
spill over the dam,
a continual effort
to feed the running
river.

Gradually that pond
has become clogged
with refuse, impoverished,
brown with longing
for the world's first day.

But it moves,
high tide or low,
and the grey carp line up
like docked submarines
in the flow, gleaning
what passes with gaping
mouths, expanding gills,
as though nothing more
was expected, or hoped for.

This fragment of time
will be held in the bones:
willows mirrored on water,
bread floating on foam,
soggy loam—live things
dying of trust.

Questions

Where do the birds go
at the end of their singing lives—
and snakes, after changing clothes
    for the last time?

What happens to fish
when the glassy water chills—
and to the spirit behind
    a tiger's burning eyes?

When wild things die
is that the end, or do they fly
to some unknown shore, leaving
    weight and substance behind?

There must be a place
for all the souls that have floated
away like milkweed down, lifted
    by the breeze.

The Great Mystery
fills me again—and I am certain
of nothing except my own breathing
    the curving sky, the sea.

Timing

When the sycamore splits its bark
    in spring, and the brown river
        overruns its banks, my skin

can never contain me. Winter
    slides from my thoughts like ice
        from a warmed roof. Music thrums

between old stars. I fly past ruins
    of nebulae, slide into black holes,
        pass the light of centuries.

Bound to earth by heaviness
    of bones, the need to breathe
        remembered air, I turn from slopes

of solitude to watch the gull
    in his holy freedom, touch each
        furrowed tree, wear a scarlet
        feather in my hair.

Soundings

Nameless, still as a soul,
the force lay buried
in last summer's grasses.
Bleached stems rose stiffly
from the masses of cold
abandoned dunes—split cleanly
at a finger's touch,
protecting the perennial
drive, struggling through
winter sand dense as stone.

Old griefs forgotten,
old lives shed, waiting
motionless the might became
a gleam of green—became
forgotten words remembered
beneath the crystalling of rain,
gently falling snow.

Our mingled tears
have made us one—
all depths revealed,
hard shells shattered
and undone.

In the Fall

Sycamore leaves
are the first to go—
dropping like tears
into dark places,
floating briefly
on shallow pond,
clogging the weir.

But maples dance,
sing with color,
shake leaves down
like tossed confetti.
Music rises
from jeweled paths.

The ancient rhythm of earth
has begun again. We see
her shed all extraneous
clothing, like a lover—
her breath slow and shallow
in sun's slanting rays.
The soul is left, bereft
of every ornament.

We all come to this:
off with earrings,
bracelets, necklaces.
Unadorned and apart
we find ourselves
close to earth's
beating heart.

Grey Day in Autumn

A ragged line of geese
skeined the sky, left
conversation floating
behind, dissolving in low
clouds. Changing leads,
flying in the wake
of each other's wings,
they spoke of homing
and myriad things known
only to their kind: marshes,
sweet grass heavy with seed,
a surge of life so strong
it stilled spirits in the air.

How did they know the sky's roads
without markers or names—
which lanes went north or south
since no stars shone to guide?
What commandments led them
into a blind sky, toward
an unknown salvation, tunnelling
into the mouth of chance?

After their voices died
I felt the loneliness
of an abandoned child,
a yearning to surrender
all my years—to stand before
a secret wilderness
where I would comprehend
the incantations of birds—
where I could easily fly.

Some, by Flood

I wonder if the earthworm
in the neutral silence
of his subterranean life
is concerned with the world turning.

Does he know enough to hide
from the tunnelling mole,
the sharp spade? Is he satisfied
with this steady diet of dirt?

If he fears anything it could be
heavy, relentless rain. Washed
to the surface he lies vulnerable
to crushing tires, scalding sun.

Eating his way through continents,
is he merely an insatiable
digesting machine, content to be
nothing more? Or does he believe

in some elysian field
where he will live forever
after his labors are through?
Do you?

If I Were Blind

yet I would see the birds
flying across the screen
of memory—no need to watch
the way they skim the skies,
crowd feeders above new snow
discussing things of great
concern, resembling a painting
done years ago.

Sometimes
I practice blindness
to meet the threat
of absolute negative light—
then allow my eyes
to capture everything
in sight.

Turtle

Cowering in the doorway,
green muddy shell slashed
halfway through, ancient
head withdrawn, hooded eyes
shut against endings,
he waited.

We filled the gash with ointment,
washed him clean, drove to
the nearby pond, placed
him gently at the shallow end.

He was not seen again.
Was he tended by caring carp,
healed by cool water,
or delivered whole
into a new dimension
of light?

Lame Deer, Seeker of Visions*

Still as a stone
he sits before
the gift of fire—
eyes holding yesterday,
spell of the *Nagi,*
power of *Keha* far away.

Knowing that mountains
are forever, and time
cannot be measured, he
drifts easily into days
of *wicasa wakan,* hearing
sound of war cry on far hills,
feeling the fading grace
of a Great Spirit upon
deep rivers of his face.

Old magic vanished—
even his way of death,
leaving only breath
to pray for power,
yearning to hear again
echoing talk of drum.

Holding his peace pipe,
strong symbol of himself,
sensing strength in the helix
of its smoke, he weeps
silently, alone,
still as a stone.

*A book by John Fire Lame Deer

At First Light

before earth
summons the sun,
a chattering begins
in an exotic tongue
dividing night from morn—
ritual of music
blooming like flowers—
bright seduction
airborne.

Without this conversation
morning would arrive
subdued, with empty hands,
no more dimensional
than grey on grey,
a silent cavalcade—
the way it was
before the birds
were made.

Space

Somewhere
beyond the Milky Way
there is music so sublime
that hearing it
could melt bone
cause blood to sing.

Sometimes
that sound
bleaches the moon
or turns it red
with longing.

Now and then
a note or two escapes
streaks toward earth
is caught
in the throat
of a wren.

Illusion

Do you think
that this is the real world:
explosions of roses,
silver-plated seas, electric
eels, pearls, rainbows,
shooting stars, the hard
bright lantern moon?

Or was all of it
dreamed one night
in a time before time?
These words fade
as I write. There are
no gods, no geography—
no day or night.

But somewhere out of sight
is an unknowable force
where awareness is measured
out and recalled, as we
warm our brief hearts
at the wonder.

One Morning in June

Let me tell you about miracles—
　　how one by one, perfect, thin
　　　　as threads the newborn mantises

emerged from their crisp womb
　　on a bayberry bush, wavered
　　　　against hard branches,

descended warily
　　onto rich grasses, measuring
　　　　the vastness of earth.

No one could count them all.
　　At once their pale green bodies
　　　　blended with the colors of summer.

What voice did they hear
　　saying *"Now"*? How many survived
　　　　in the blinding light?

When the last one disappeared
　　I turned away with a feeling of grace
　　　　that lasted for days.

Animus

Something waits
    beneath packed earth
        the measureless sea

waits within
    a clenched clam
        the hibernating eel

within a bird's breast
    a tree's heart
        the perennial fern

the grey grinding ice
    a curled leaf
        an exhausted moon

something waits
    unnamed, invisible,
        silent as snow

waits to spring
    waits impatiently
        in me.

Natural History

Natural History

Crazy old lady, we said,
watching her shuffle down the road,
balancing on sailor's legs, hearing
her raucous imitation of crows.
Even on warm days she wore a winter cap
over rope-grey hair, patched dungarees,
frayed coat. Unsteady in strong wind
she faced the bay, waved at gulls,
smiled at secrets. Her red-rimmed eyes
searched the heavens for some expected sign.

Full of green years and mischief
we trailed along, mimicked her rolling gait,
give and take of bird talk—scorned her
from our pinnacle of youth.

Today, hearing wind scour the sky,
I donned my knitted hat, old brown sweater,
began my daily pilgrimage to see
the clam boats heading home, hear
soft drag and whisper of the tide,
taste sea air. Behind me children snickered
as I spoke to mockers, answered a cardinal's call.
She thinks she's a bird, they said, laughing
into the twisting sky.

Stumbling toward home
I felt the tears begin—
blamed them on the sharp
salt wind.

Other Places, Other Lives

In summer I awake bemused—
gaze overlong at dancing trees,
scudding clouds, rippling water.
Cicadas lull me with their
metamorphosed harmony, until
I have become the silent mist,
a vine in lacy branches, the power
within a whale.

Returning from nirvana
is certain as breathing,
startling as sudden sound—
from sweet freedom to measured
time, where a flower is nothing
more than itself, a tree
a common earthbound sight.

But one lingering note
from wind chimes and I am
mutable as the moon,
a Buddhist on a mountain
in Tibet, charged with light!

Incidentals

Because of our sins
the possum died—lay
heart-stopped on the snaking
road, his grey coat silver
with morning mist. All
he had wanted to do
was cross the street—his
as much as ours.

The assassin sped away
in his bloodred car. I saw
him toss a beer can from
the window. Sound of furious
music stung the air. Tires flung
pebbles backward like bird shot.

I picked up the lifeless form,
wrapped it in an old shirt.
Feeling there should be words
I said *forgive us our trespasses*
and buried him.

Sorcery

All of it depends
on the full, aching moon.
There might be
a high keening
over the waters—
magnetic, irresistible.
Wearing white, renouncing
everything, smiling
at the covetous night
I stride into the beckoning
sea with such high courage
no one would believe
it had ever occurred
to me. Breathing silence,
perfectly composed,
I offer myself
to another century.

When dawn, pale, thin,
edges the world
I wake to find
a shred of seaweed
on my skin.

Tonic

Old, tired, aching
in back and knees
I dragged myself
to the couch, slouched
onto faded pillows
with a tepid cup of tea,
turned on TV.
"Juke Box Saturday Night"
flooded the room.
The Andrews Sisters,
fabulous as ever, sang
"Don't Sit Under the Apple Tree."

Electrified, light as air,
twice twenty years dismissed,
I sprang to my feet, drawn
into the old mad dance, sang
every word of every song,
caught in the familiar groove
of *my* youth, *my* beat.

Later, out of breath,
sane, replete with power,
I rearranged those martyred
bones in comfortable recline,
still breathing flame!

Carousel

When I was five or six
or seven, I thought heaven
was a merry-go-round. Climbing
onto my sturdy horse, waiting
for the music to fall around me
like sunlight, I held tight
to the gleaming pole, longing
for the ride to begin.
And up and forward and down
we surged, traveling miles
in that magical circle
until I was dizzy with joy,
unwilling to let go
when the platform stilled.

Today, if I could find
a carousel, I would again
ascend that painted charger,
feel him come to life beneath
me, canceling the years;
not caring if people laughed—
said, look at that crazy lady
who thinks she's young again!
Coming around for the tenth time
I'd see them turning toward
the ticket booth, exchanging
currency for nostalgia, envy
for unbridled bliss.

Sanctuary

Campfires
were my altars then—
sparks turned to prayers,
floated high, became stars.
Faith lay in things seen:
night with its arms friendly
about our shoulders; red
glow of grey driftwood
burning down, pulsing the air,
melting sand to crystals
reflecting forever and ever.

That was all. My world
encompassed a small place.
When the fire died we sang
an ancient hymn, said good night,
brushed the beach from our feet,
believing all the words ever said
about love.

Bonsai

Root pruned, twisted, branches
thwarted in vain attempt to grow,
turning its energy inward, the cedar
crouches, reaching sideways, grasping
small avenues of air.

Visiting an ancient friend,
her pale eyes closed against
alien walls, I saw parchment hands
curled in upon themselves, legs
weak as dry sticks, the relic
of her strength drawn within.
When she spoke her words reached
backward into yesterday.

Hurrying home, I released
that dwarfed imprisoned tree,
spread its tortured roots,
planted it in loose warm soil
in my garden, facing south.

Jasmine

is laced with cunning
and waxy bloom. Its
midnight scent
enters the blood
like a veiled dream:

I am in Cathay
on a teeming avenue.
Vendors offer savory delights.
I stride, lithe and sinuous
in golden sandals and a white
silk gown. Sloe eyed, exotic,
I own a smile so dazzling
that strangers stop, stare,
become my retinue.
The moon-pull of desire
is raw and sweet.
The whole deep river
of the world is mine,
and I am swept away
in its sensuous tide.

I wake to a trail of blossoms
on my face. Night's firestorm
dissolves without a trace.

Galloping Horse of Kansu

captured completely:
the artful tilt of head,
arch of neck, proud flowing
tail, the perfect split-second
balance on one hind leg, part
of a prance into history.
Mouth agape, breathing fire
and blue air, you have been
caught forever in the absolute
joy of being.

Energy from your body
flows into mine—the unbearable
happiness of flight. I see you
move through summer fields
of green grasses, hear
your laughter, wild and free,
feel the thunder of your running,
and imagine the blessing
of a soft kiss on my hand
as I feed you an apple offering.

You spoke to me
the moment we met—
moving, unmoving, another
Pegasus leaping toward
morning, able to fly!

Chanel No. 5

promises me the world.
One drop behind each ear
and I am long limbed,
satin gowned, languorous,
seductive, perfectly poised.
A fiery, intense, handsome
Italian in formal dress
(obviously my slave)
bends over my manicured
fingers ready to whisk
me away to joys unknown.
Sensuous, irresistible,
I rise gracefully
from the velvet couch.
He drapes me in sable,
I smile, we saunter
to the Rolls.

My roughened gardener's hands
catch on the kitchen towel;
a faded reflection observes me
from the bright frying pan.
But still I dance around
the room—believing implicitly
in the power of that three
hundred dollar an ounce
perfume!

Saying Good-Bye

Surrounded by packed cartons,
drapeless windows, blank walls,
we watch the sun set over the river,
its rays turning skies crimson,
clouds shredding and glinting
in its afterglow; the tide
coming in, rippling under the Canadas
bearing north; clam boats veering
into their home slips; black dogs
standing like statues on the prows.
We hear the soft slap of small waves
worrying wet sand, bathing the bulkhead.
A sailboat shifts in scarlet waters.
Soundless, the sun drowns in gunmetal
seas, draining the sentient clouds.

We turn away before saying good-bye,
before things finalize, become true.
I'll call, you promise, and I am blind
with tears and cannot answer, and so
pretend the slipstream sun is all
to blame, the winter heat of it
having seared my eyes. Diminished
by change I hurry away, wishing to be
mindless, unaware, like the everlasting
unaffected tide.

Dimensions

In the ebb tide
    of just before dreaming,
        those tenuous moments

when shadows roam
    where nothing is strange,
        words surface easily

sliding like silk through the mind
    arranging themselves into ballads,
        sonnets, villanelle

glossy as gold. I know
    that I should light the lamp,
        give form to this glowing

composition. Instead, weary,
    drifting away, I vow
        to remember every line.

But, of course, by morning
    the shining has fled
        back to the cosmic chaos

disappeared down corridors
    of night. Am I being teased
        by the lasting dream

of doing one thing, in all my life,
    perfectly—the way the world turns
        perfectly, every single day?

The Garden House

You never know,
he often said,
when an old washer,
that length of wire,
a tangled fishing line
might come in handy.

Which means
that shelves were full
of cracked clay pots,
an old chipped saw, rope
like uncoiled snakes,
tins of congealed paint,
jars of rusted nails.

When he left, what remained
was not in the earthy smell
of his clothes, the desk
where he paid bills,
his hairbrush on the sill,
a bottle of prescription pills.

When need drives me,
I go to the garden house
where all the fragments lay—
and close the door, hoping that
some force of memory will bring
him near, smiling his crooked smile,
hanging up his garden cap, saying
it must be time for lunch, hon,
and I will hug him fiercely
as before. You never know.

Return to Cutchogue
for Laura

They said she was bemused
by sun dancing on the sea,
smell of eelgrass ribboning the shore—

or that entranced, she gazed too long
at mirrored images of docks and sails—
gulls flying through water, trees rooted in sky.

Perhaps the nearness of stars
wheeling through deep-set nights
kindled flecks of fire in her eyes.

Some unknown alchemy, siren songs, a spell,
elixir from a golden cup, had worked
their sorcery—erased the years between.

I have my own idea: she heard
her children's voices singing on the wind,
their laughter changed to jingle shells,
dazzling the sand.

In the Genes

Is it blood memory,
something fashioned in the bone,
that holds me hostage to a love
of the infinitely vulnerable,
infinitely small—the shy arbutus,
a fallen leaf, the treasure
of a tear? I tremble with
a strange compassion that is
not mine, divided into sudden
action, laughter, fear.

What daydream finds me hungering
for one vision that is mine alone,
stamping itself across an empty page,
leaving behind the worn-out cords
of ancestry, to let me stand upon
a wild and magic stage, free as air?

But I am bound by silken threads
of old fables, sacramental songs,
stitched samplers on forgotten walls—
my mother's smile, my father's hands.

Is there nothing of my very own,
unbounded, born of liberty?
Is there nothing of Eve in me?

A Week in the Woods

One week in thick woods
and I am filled with other
languages, hold conversations
with ferns and flowers,
gossip with birds.

Walking on pine needles
spongy with damp moss
and the sudden assertion
of Indian pipes, I breathe
air so sweet it transforms me
into some new being, someone
ancient, a worshipper of trees,
one who follows bees to the hive,
walks with soundless feet
swift as running streams.
I touch rocks with reverence,
live on wine of berries, sleep
in nested leaves, wash in rain.

One week
and I no longer fit
in the treacherous forked-tongue
world of men—the world of before,
the world of then.

My Father

Since we were
nearly strangers
when he left,
it seems a revelation
he is here now
in my hands, holding
pen or sable brush,
or with my eyes
worshipping the sea.

All I can recall
of him are images—
far distant—which
could have happened
in another century:
our strolls in woods
"to see what we shall see,"
sun patterning his hair,
shoulder warm as he
carried me home,
silky mustache
tickling my cheek.

But now, suddenly,
he's become a part of me.
We listen together
to the arias of birds,
hum of bees—I laugh
with his laughter,
write words he might
have said. To think
that for sixty empty years
I could have imagined him
dead!

Living with Ghosts

What invisible cord connects me
to an orange bowl filled with blue
plums on a white table in an old
house where I haven't lived for years?
Did Cézanne paint from memory?

How do I remember tendrils
of curls escaping my mother's
long brown hair, as she wound
those tresses into a tidy bun?
Did Renoir paint from life?

What compartment of my brain
remembers green tips of asparagus
emerging stout and strong from
warm soil—ripe peaches
on an oft-climbed tree—
a sheet-draped tricycle, red as fire,
awaiting my fifth birthday?
Did Klee dream of wheels?

And this most vivid scene:
my gentle, bloodless father
breathing his last soft breaths
in a brass bed, under white sheets,
gazing with closed eyes
into the near horizon of eternity.
And the indelible moving picture
of strangers lowering him
into earth's dark center,
and how it shattered the still life
of my world.

The Zwieback Tree

Part of me
still lives
in an old house
on a short street
called Edgewood Court.

The corner lot is vacant
and in its center stands
a great wide tree we call
the zwieback tree. Laughing,
we stand beneath it, holding
out our arms, trying to catch
the sweet brown toast
raining from high branches.

Later, when we learned
how a freckled boy
with magic in his mind
played summer Santa,
it didn't change a thing.
Accustomed to fairy tales,
we believed.

Though that square ground
holds houses now, I am haunted
by a tree, still rooted
in my mind, gnarled and leafy,
shaking down rusks, holding
secrets, connecting me
by slender thread
to the child,
to fantasy.

Courtship Dance

The crane dips and bows,
turning, showing his best side
before his chosen mate, shifting
feet, stretching his long neck,
saying, See me? I'm the one—
handsome, tall, full-feathered,
at my best age and dress.
If she agrees, they cross bills
as emphasis, and hurry away.

You come to my door, hair shining,
wearing Sunday clothes, teeth
gleaming behind come-hither smiles,
teasing me with your ocean eyes.
I hear the sound of music. Drawn
together by an unseen force
we discover the same inland sea—
a private edge of sky.

Belle Meade Road

Traffic thrums and blares. A gold-coin
sun, pure but vengeful, stares at the noon
departure of workers and patients
from red-brick buildings where the lame,
the halt, the bandaged, of which I am one,
emerge like casualties of war. In twos
and threes we cautiously cross between cars
through the thick hot air toward the deli
whose windows blink in neon announcing
"Cold Beer."

Out in front, tables blooming with striped
umbrellas, skirted by curved benches,
invite and beckon, offering healing shade.

The oval patio, girdled by a raised
garden, is edged with flat stones forming
a low wall. Shrubs and flowers choke
in the gas-fumed air.

Suddenly, amidst laughter, chatter,
the stiff and lively smell of hotdogs
and mustard, whizz of traffic, a chipmunk
ventures forth from a chink in the wall
to steal a fallen crumb. Then disappears.

We both dodge life's hazards, surface
from our separate lairs for sustenance,
feel in our hearts the wild joy
of survival.

The Mind's Eye

I remember yellow birds
    flying like living ornaments
        through waving trees

wildflowers bursting into flame
    sycamores stretching in sun
        splitting their skins

stars zigzagging through
    summer skies, minnows
        rippling tides.

I need to look closely again
    at blundering bees on zinnias
        inchworms measuring my hand

the carnival of autumn.
    Now there is a longing in me
        for the simple feeling of joy

the first clear vision of a child
    the way I once saw
        every living thing.

The Dance

Beguiled by the beat
of a popular song, we lived
a transient love affair
lasting forever
though we had never met
before.

Is there a name for it—
an inward delight so complete
it can never be spoken?
Flawless together, we were
two halves of a whole,
harmonious, soul to soul.

Everyone marveled
at the way we appeared—
pledged for life,
partners for years.

Remembering,
I feel light as down,
perfect again.
The moment glows
like poured red wine
in the sun.

Secrets

What planes of existence lie
behind a cat's eyes? Those
measuring slits of light
strip me of pretense, dismiss
my command as I edge him from
tabletop to floor. What mystery
passes between us as our eyes hold?
I feel pinned by their relentless
cryptic stare. Merciless in their
scrutiny, they total my mistakes
with cool superior reason,
drain whatever power I possess.

I am spellbound before
their everlastingness.

Overture to Pearl Harbor

My nineteenth year. That boy!
His crisp blond hair, smiling lips
inviting mine. Ocean eyes one could
drown in, write poems about. The new
pink angora sweater I wore one night
that left itself all over his dark
jacket. How we laughed about that!

Then the parting, flame and ashes,
as he left for Purdue. His calls,
sweet wonder, filling empty days.
And love, stretching on warmed wires
between us. Promises of forever,
whose face we could not see. Letters
lying against my heart to still the ache.

Soon, rumors of war: bombed ships
sinking like stones. How could we
know that time runs out, ends abruptly
in the dust of some far-off land—
that forever is just a melody
that fades and twists into a word
called never?

As Usual

At the dentist's office teeth are being drilled.
Police patrol their designated streets.
We are instructed to have a good day
by cashiers at every marketplace.
Radios blare, horns honk, balloons burst,
clocks chime, classes convene. Trucks thunder
down highways. Traffic lights blink on and off.

Birds soar below shifting clouds. The surge
of life beneath dead grasses waits to be reborn.
A benign sun stares, swinging low in a bland sky.
Snow melts, tides change, winds move lingering
leaves. Flickers appear and depart from feeders.
Willows wave languidly, refusing to change
the color of their hair.

And half the world away missiles rise
swiftly in desert air. Bombs fall
with bruising regularity. Skies explode.
Sanity recedes. Hatreds flare.

And I am sick with longing
for something elusive
called love.

The English Patient*

Let me paint a tableau
from page three: the patient's
burnt body, brown as leather,
spread-eagled across an iron cot;
candlelight flickering on a white
table; the nurse, seated beside him,
squeezing the red juice of a purple plum
into the dark cavern of his mouth;
indigo sky falling through
the fractured roof of an abandoned
villa in Italy.

But how shall I paint despair,
madness of war, anticipation
of death, the end of hope?
What is the color of air?

My palette—burnt umber
with variations. And the two
of them fading into night
the way my memories of war
have dimmed, but kept alive
by the white-hot embers
of remembrance.

*A novel by Michael Ondaatje

Raggedy Woman

On the killing streets of Manhattan—
specifically, the corner of 6th and 50th,
the bloated old woman sat like an island
amid a surging stream of humanity,
the street pole and a tilting chair
her only visible means of support.
A crushed fedora settled low over wisps
of white hair, an ulcerated leg ballooned
on a splintered throwaway crate.

Surrounded by shopping bags stuffed
with old clothes, a toaster trailing
its cut umbilical cord, the neck of a bottle
rising like a voice out of the debris,
her presence became a still point
in a festering city—cacophony for company.

"How ya doin', Rosie?" a passing peddler
asked. Hurrying by, I turned in time
to see her raise one trembling arm,
fingers split in the victory sign.

Dusk

Men, animals, fish
    are going blind
        at the southern end of Chile

because of a hole
    in the sky, letting through
        hard ultraviolet rays.

Air is green with gasses
    veiling a struggling sun—
        we wear masks to breathe.

Water is laced with poisons.
    Cancer claims one in nine.
        AIDS runs rampant.

The gouged earth groans,
    unable to sustain
        its vital heart.

The carved-out moon,
    sharp as a scimitar,
        defines night,

attempts to feel compassion
    for this graceless world—
        fails, moves on.

December Storm, 1993

The storm begins with light
innocent snow, evolves into
sudden sleet, howling winds
leveling trees, sting of ice
against windows, dark and sodden
skies. Tides rise, inch by inch,
claiming the dock, the walk,
the patio. A swollen bay
finds its way to a rendezvous
with an arm of itself
on the disappearing street.
Barometers plunge.

We tape windows, fill oil lamps,
search for candles, fill the firebox
with logs, feel the cold clutch
of fear—pretend indifference.

When the driveway disappears
I shall sit in the shower stall,
close the door,
and sing.

When My Time Comes

I shall depart in style:
off-the-shoulder short-sleeved
chartreuse blouse, black leather
miniskirt, up to here,
low-slung double Che Guevara
belt (with real bullets),
snakeskin boots heavy with chains
that clank and jingle
(or would if I could walk),
twenty glittering bracelets
on each arm, flashing rings
stiffening my fingers
(thumbs included),
hair dyed flaming red
twisted into spikes,
mascara thick as tar
imprisoning my eyes,
lipstick the color of venous
blood on my sensuous mouth,
nails crimson, sharp,
perilously long.

As I lay there, with it, serene,
people will gasp and say
they never really knew me.
I shall take along the power
and the glory of a hard-rock
song—the whole fantastic
messed-up freaked-out century.

About the Author

Lynn Kozma, a retired registered nurse, served in World War II. She is the author of one book of poetry, *Catching the Light* (Pocahontas Press, 1989), and one poetry chapbook, *Great South Bay* (Birnham Wood Graphics, 1993). Her work is included in *When I Am an Old Woman I Shall Wear Purple* (Papier-Mache Press, 1987) and *If I Had My Life to Live Over I Would Pick More Daisies* (Papier-Mache Press, 1992), and she has been published often by *Midwest Poetry Review, Bitterroot, Long Island Quarterly*, and *The Lyric*. She is an avid reader, gardener, and birder. A continuing student at Suffolk Community College, she is a member of Poets & Writers, Inc.

Quality Books from Papier-Mache Press

At Papier-Mache Press our goal is to produce attractive, accessible books that deal with contemporary personal, social, and political issues. Our titles have found an enthusiastic audience in general interest, women's, new age, and religious bookstores, as well as in gift stores, mail order catalogs, and libraries. Many of our books have also been used by teachers for women's studies, creative writing, and gerontology classes, and by therapists and family counselors to help clients explore personal issues such as aging and relationships.

If you are interested in finding out more about our titles, ask your local bookstores which Papier-Mache items they carry. Or, if you would like to receive a complete catalog of books, posters, and shirts from Papier-Mache Press, please send a self-addressed stamped envelope to:

Papier-Mache Press
135 Aviation Way, #14
Watsonville, CA 95076